# The Lazy Pharmacist's Way to Wealth

## How not to rely on the Government

# Lynda Chanin
BPharm. (Bath)

. . . . .

Proof and Additional Material by
Christopher Chanin
B.Sc. (Bioch. Lon.)
B.Sc (Pharm. Liverp.)

. . . . .

Cover Design, Print & ePUB Layout by
N.D. Author Services [NDAS]
www.NDAuthorServices.com

# Dedication

To Christopher,
my soul mate and support
in business and in life.

# Contents

LYNDA CHANIN

# Foreword

If you are struggling to make any serious profit in your pharmacy...
If you have tried to cut costs and are still not making ends meet...
If you are fed up with theories that don't work...
Then:

This is the book you've been waiting for—maybe for so long. I've known Lynda and Chris Chanin for over 20 years and have found them to be so dedicated in their desire to help their clients succeed in their businesses.

They understand that small independent business owners, just like you, have so many jobs to do that it's difficult to know where your energies should be best applied. You'll find this book is written in such an "easy to follow" format; full of simple suggestions that, when applied, can make your business more profitable, allowing you far more time to balance your work and home commitments.

My suggestion: read it now!

—Peter Thomson, "The UK's Leading Strategist on Business and Personal Growth"

LYNDA CHANIN

# Introduction

"Many a small thing has been made
large by the right kind of advertising."
—Mark Twain
(Pen name of American author
Samuel Langhorne Clemens,
1835 to 1910)

Marketing is the main area that most community pharmacies struggle with and yet it is the one that will increase your business most cost effectively. All businesses need to market to survive and you will notice how much the bigger companies advertise even though they are earning millions already.

The first thing is to ensure your pharmacy is the best it can be, particularly in terms of service. Marketing will bring customers to your door but being excellent will keep them coming back. Then use as many different ways of marketing as you can. If you only open the front door then you are vulnerable if another pharmacy opens up or your surgery moves away. If you have several streams of marketing, you will reach your customers regardless.

Think about your customers and what they are most likely to want to buy. If your population is largely elderly then running offers on baby items is not going to increase your sales whilst marketing Tena lady to the under 30's is unlikely to boost turnover. Ensure that you are still maintaining a decent profit margin on your offer stock. Always remember these wise words:

> Turnover is vanity,
> Profit is sanity and
> Cashflow is reality.

This means that you should not drive your business by script count alone. It is eminently possible to pick up scripts which cost you money to dispense! Know the net profit on everything you do, and try not to pay for the stock until you have sold your goods and got the cash in the bank.

## Word of Mouth

Word of mouth is indeed very powerful. However, it relies on an accurate understanding on the part of the client passing on "the Word" of all the good things you do, that perhaps many other pharmacies do not. Your client may only be aware of the small number of services he/she actually uses. If you make a change for the better in one of those services, then your passer-on may well not be aware of those changes. They may not have been in your shop for a couple of months.

Word of mouth is also very slow—but it can be kick started by marketing, which itself is not instantaneous .

If you maintain social media contact with them, you can tell them of improvements as soon as they are made.

Marketers call social media "Word of mouth on Steroids".

Marketing rarely leads to an immediate increase in income, unless you can afford a high profile TV advertising campaign, but by being persistent you will establish familiarity with your customers and your business will thrive, especially as so few of your competitors will be marketing.

Concentrate on one area at a time and getting it running smoothly before you start to tackle the next one. Work out what you want to achieve through your marketing and how you are going to measure your results. If you don't measure them you will not know if you have reached your target or not, or whether your marketing is cost effective.

Start with the free stuff like eMailing, Facebook and window displays before moving on to the more costly ways like direct mail and space advertising.

# Chapter One:
# Space Advertising

"Doing business without advertising
is like winking at a girl in the dark.
You know what you are doing, but
nobody else does."
—Stuart H Britt
(US advertising executive)

"The man who stops advertising to
save money is like the man who
stops the clock to save time."
—Thomas Jefferson
(Third president of the
United States of America)

## 1. Which Newspaper or Magazine Should We Advertise in?

When thinking about space advertising the first thing to consider is what magazine or newspaper is going to be the most cost effective for you. A national paper or magazine will be very expensive so unless you have a number of branches throughout the country it probably isn't the best option.

So we are looking at local magazines or papers. Now do you have one in your area that is a daily paid one or have you only got local freebies? The point here is that people tend not to appreciate anything that is free, so if they have paid for the paper/magazine they are more likely to read it and therefore see your advert. On the other hand a weekly freebie will go to every household in your area and will probably hang around the house for at least a week, so there may be more chance it is read.

The price of the advert may be a factor. The only way you can really know for certain is to run the exact same ads in the paid and free papers and compare the response rate with the money you paid for the advert. You do this by coding each advert and explaining to potential customers that they have to quote the code. You need to set up a system so you can capture that information easily. Customers often do not remember the code or cut out and bring in the advert.

## 2. Where

The next question is where in the magazine/paper should you put the advert? It is generally agreed that the nearer the front of the paper the better unless of course your target audience is men in which case the nearer to the back page the better. It does sound a bit stereotypical but men seem to be more interested in reading about sport than women.

The right page is likely to get more attention than the left because most people are right-handed so as they flick through the paper they tend to look at those more. Also the bottom and outside space is seen more than the left or upper areas. So your best bet is the bottom right hand corner as close to the front as you can, if you are aiming for a smaller advert.

Repeating a smaller advert on the same page or on several different pages can get more response than a larger advert. People notice it more. You may remember the "Eucerin" adverts in the C&D which were on three consecutive outer right hand pages. I suspect most of us spotted them.

## 3. Pre-Headline

This can often be a short sentence to improve targeting of the reader. For example "Have you been thinking about giving up smoking?"

In space adverts the Pre-Headline is usually a really good image. Pictures attract attention and the ones that get most noticed are those of humans, especially faces. Use a good picture of yourself or a member of staff if you can. After faces people notice cute puppies and kittens. Can you weave any of these pictures into your advert?

People will always look at the picture first and then their eye travels down the page, which is why the headline must always be put below the picture. Hence the picture is an ideal Pre-Headline.

Coloured pictures are much better than black and white, so if you can possibly afford it use 4 colour.

## 4. Headline

The purpose of the headline is to grab the reader's attention and be interesting enough so they will read the first paragraph. It's the "advert for the advert".

The headline must be eye catching and clear. Having a funny headline, or one that people have to think about, is not going to hold people's attention or encourage them to come to your pharmacy to buy something. Humour is very subjective, and is usually best avoided.

Think what is the best part of the offer you are making and put that in the headline. So if it is a buy one get one free, say so in the headline or a free NRT product to help them stop smoking, it goes in the headline. Make the head line emotional rather than just factual e.g. "Desperate to Stop Smoking—Join Our Scheme and Get FREE Patches, Gum or Lozenges".

This headline is designed to attract the attention of just those most likely to sign up. Another example would be: "Want to Drop Two or Three Dress Sizes- Try our New diet!". Both of these would be ignored by people who don't smoke or don't need to lose weight but they are not going to be interested in what you are offering anyway.

Don't put the whole headline in capitals as people find that difficult to read. Just use capitals on the main words and keep to the same font as the body copy though you may want to change the colour to make it more noticeable.

Put inverted commas around the headline as this makes the headline more eye catching.

# 5. Copy

The body copy is those lines under the headline that explain the details of your offer and the benefits of it to your clients. Like all the other writing we have been discussing it should be aimed at the average reading age of 8. Short sentences, short paragraphs and simple concepts.

One way to write, if you are not an expert copy writer, is just to put down everything you want to say about the product/service you are advertising, leave it for a day or so and then go back over it to make it much sharper. Remove wasted words and phrases and make sure it says what you intended it to say.

Another good way of writing a great advert is to Copy someone else's Writing. This is the essence of copy writing. There is no point in "re-inventing the wheel" each time. Choose an advert that has been proven to sell and adopt and adapt it to what you want to say now.

Make sure the copy states the benefits to the clients, as well as features of the product or service and that the main offer is unambiguous.

# 6. Call to Action

Don't ever write an advert and leave out the call to action. The call to action can be as simple as ORDER NOW, giving a single choice of what to do and who to contact. People find it difficult to make a decision so given a choice may end up doing nothing.

# 7. Coupons

Cut out coupons are always a good idea. They become a simple way of keeping track of which advert the client was responding to. You place the coupon at the bottom of the advert. Repeat the offer in the coupon i.e. "Yes I would like to drop a dress size by using the Euro diet" then have a space for their details and a code on the coupon so you know which paper they cut the coupon from.

Use dotted lines around the edge to show the client that they should cut out the coupon. Use a clip art of a pair of scissors so it's clear the customer cuts it out and finally give details of what they should do with it i.e. post it to..., fax it to..., phone us quoting... or bring it in....

# 8. Negotiation with the Newspaper

It is important to realise that you can negotiate rates with the newspapers. The advertising space is a time limited commodity. If they have not managed to sell it by the time it goes to print they can never get that money back. So you have a certain amount of power in these discussions.

We found that when we first approached the local paper and tried to negotiate we got very little response but once we mentioned that we had a prepared advert in a form that they could use straight away they became more interested. After a period of time they would regularly contact us to explain that they had a full page right hand side 5 pages in at 20% of the price they normally charge. Obviously the more you use them the more they are open to doing deals.

One way to tempt the newspaper to use your advert, if it is not too time sensitive, is to send the ad as well as a cheque for what you want to pay, with a message saying "if you have a gap you can't fill cash the cheque and use this ad".

# 9. Who?

Do not let somebody who writes for the newspaper write your advert for you. The chances are the person who is given the job does not know how to write a good space advert. He may simply be employed to sell the advertising that is needed to make the paper pay or the type setter who sets out the layout of the advertising on the pages.

He will have no interest in getting the best result for your advert and will probably be designing a number of adverts for several different companies. Most of these companies will not record the results they achieve through their advertising, so there is no way the people working for the paper will know what works and what doesn't.

If you are not sure how to set an advert, even after reading this book then contact somebody who does it for a living. As in anything when you are looking for an expert, ask for testimonials from satisfied clients before you waste your money.

The Informacist.com employs experienced copywriters, so we could probably help you. Call us to find out how much we would charge: 0151-653-3115.

# Chapter Two: eMail

"Imagine you are writing an email. You are in front of the computer. You are operating the computer, clicking a mouse and typing on a keyboard, but the message will be sent to a human over the internet. So you are working before the computer, but with a human behind the computer."
—Yukihiro Matsumoto
(Chief Architect of Ruby at Heroku, an online cloud service in San Francisco)

## 1. Have a Subject for Your eMail; It's Your Advert for Your eMail

As in ALL marketing put something in the "subject" box at the top of the email that is short but interesting enough to make your customer want to open it. Think about what would do to attract your customers—usually it will be a way of saving money or to get some information e.g. 5 tips for avoiding catching a cold this winter, Buy one get one free on Joe Bloggs deodorant, etc.

It is a good idea to include the client's first name in the subject line as there are few things more eye-catching than your own name.

## 2. Headline

You then need a headline to catch the clients eye once they open the email. Away motivated head lines tend to work better than towards motivated. This involves talking about a problem they might have and then explaining that you have a solution. Put your best solution to the problem in the headline.

## 3. Body Copy

Create body copy that will inspire your clients to purchase something from you. Body copy is the main bulk of the email after the salutation. As with direct mail, you should think about what the product or service you are advertising will do for your clients. Will it save them time or money, keep them healthy or make them beautiful?

Explain how much time and money it could save, how it will help keep them healthy or make them beautiful. Having testimonials from other customers, who have found the product/service helpful or using the ratings that some magazines do, is always a good idea.

Then don't forget to finish with the call to action i.e. telling them how to order generally by giving as few options as is practical, e.g. phoning you or visiting your webshop. Don't just use the words "order now". Research has shown a better response if you write something like "yes I would like to enjoy the same benefits so many others are, by ordering......."

## 4. Have a system

Once you start emailing on a regular basis you need to have a system that will keep a track of who you have sent emails to, who opened them and who ordered in response to them. In order to do this you will need a CRM (customer relationship management) system. There are several different companies that do this but our research has found "Goldmine" to be the most useful as it is the best supported, most user friendly and with the best range of features.

The more information you can record on your database about your patients the more you can build up a picture of their purchasing habits, their family, income, health issues etc. so you can begin to tailor the products you stock and the services you offer to your clients.

# 5. eMail Regularly

Email on a regular basis. As with all marketing, it is persistence that pays. So set up systems that will send out emails on a monthly or quarterly timetable. It is better to start with fewer and then send the email more often, than having to decrease the frequency because you cannot cope.

Start with a manageable number of customers. say 20 or 50. This way it is not too much work to begin with and you can gain experience in the things that work and things that don't at your own pace. You have to be careful when you are emailing that you don't send all your emails at once because if you mail more than say 10 people at a time the spam filters will pick it up and the email will be instantly transferred to everybody's spam box. and all your efforts will have been wasted.

The CRM systems that we mentioned earlier, have ways around this problem so you can send out large groups of emails that do not get transferred to the spam boxes.

There are a number of websites which specialise in emailing to a list which you provide. We have experience of one called Mailchimp.com.

# 6. Send Something Useful

Make sure you include something useful in all your emails. You are asking your clients to spend some of their valuable time reading your emails and the more useful they find them the more likely they are to open the next one.

As we have mentioned before the two main uses of the internet are to save money and to gain information though saving time and energy are becoming increasingly important as well. It is much easier for people to go on line after they come home from work to order items, that are often cheaper, and then have them delivered.

# 7. Get it read

Get your email read. This is one of the main problems with using emails. As there is now so much traffic on the internet people get very quickly overwhelmed by the number of items in their "in box", especially as quite a few people do not open their emails for days and sometimes weeks.

So how do you increase the likelihood of your mail getting read? The first thing is to ensure you have the correct email address. Email addresses are quite complicated and can easily be written down incorrectly so always double check. Then make sure you have written something that is eye catching and relevant in the "subject" box. This also reduces the likelihood of the email being dumped as spam.

Don't attach anything to your email. When people are trying to introduce viruses into the web system, they will put them in attachments so people are very wary of opening any of these. It also reduces the likelihood of the email being seen as spam. Finally avoid having active HTML links in the email for the same reasons.

## 8. Why Use eMail?

Use email as much as you can. It means that you can send personalised information for free so your marketing costs are greatly reduced whilst you are still creating an ongoing relationship with your clients. Much as in direct mail, you have to make the subject something that will be of interest to your clients and have a response mechanism so you can track the results.

Be aware that much email traffic will be dumped in the spam box so think carefully about using exclamation marks and words like "free". Use F'REE instead. There is also a big problem with the word "pharmacy" as so many companies trying to sell Viagra and penis enlargements over the net use the term.

All these things will make it more likely your email will end up in the spam box but creating a good headline in the subject box may help to prevent that.

## 9. Collecting Data

Collecting email addresses is fundamental to using the medium. The best way to do this is to run competitions in store where the clients fill in a credit card size form that asks for their name, address, email address and telephone number. These cards are then put into a box from which at some later date a local celebrity will make the draw.

You can use this as a piece of PR by sending the information to the local paper, especially if you were raising money for the local charity they support at the same time. If this is the case make sure the prize(s) you are offering is a good one e.g. talk to local businesses like a restaurant so they may offer a meal for two in return for the advertising you will provide or the florist so they will send flowers etc. (See Chapter 8 on holding EVENTS in your pharmacy.)

# 10. Data Storage

Once you have your names and eMails the best way to store them is in an Excel spreadsheet. This can be exported to Mailchimp. If you are going to use a CRM product you can export directly to a spreadsheet and then on to Mailchimp.

If you wish to use the simpler version of this (i.e. the spreadsheet) we have a template you can use for this.

# Chapter Three: Direct Mail

"In marketing I've seen only one strategy that can't miss—and that is to market to your best clients first, your best prospects second and the rest of the world last."
—John Romero
(Co-founder of ID Software and lead designer in *Wolfenstein 3D*, *Doom* and *Quake*)

## Make Your Direct Mail Personalised

Make your mailings personalised to your clients. You can use your PMR database if you are initially advertising an NHS service but you must have the option on the letter for the patients to state they no longer wish to receive your mail. If you are not marketing an NHS service you may need to run a competition to collect names and addresses. By the way collection and delivery services are not part of the NHS so names and addresses recorded in this way can be used to advertise non NHS services.

# Send your Direct Mail Regularly

Writing regularly to your clients will gradually build your relationship with them so in their mind you will become "their pharmacist". At any one time only about 3% of the population will be in the market for the products that you are selling. Some will be thinking about buying shortly and some in a little while. On the other hand some will not have even thought about it and some will definitely not want it because they have just bought.

By sending information at least quarterly you will hopefully catch them as the merry-go-round of life puts them in the position of wanting the product or service you are marketing. Also when they need health products and advice, your pharmacy will pop into their mind first.

## Always Make an Offer

Make an offer whenever you send a letter to your clients. It should be something that would be to their advantage like a special price, a new service, especially if it is for free because it is funded by the NHS, or a new product. You will need to find one really good offer a least a couple of weeks before you market it.

To do this, you or somebody you employ needs to keep an eye out for good offers from the wholesalers you deal with. If you/they study the price lists that you receive carefully or visit local ware-houses on a regular basis, you/they will spot cost prices that will give you a good margin and still be a very good of-fer to your clients. Remember you do not have to sell at the price the whole-saler recommends. If they are selling to you at say 50p and recommended retail price of 89p but you believe you could sell it at £1.99p buy one get one free (BOGOF) then go for it. Always check the retail price of your competitors to ensure you do not get a reputation for being very expensive but research has shown that with most clients visiting your pharmacy, cost is not their prime motivator.

## Always Provide Useful Information

Provide information that is useful to your readers as well as information relating to an offer. The simplest way to do this is with a newsletter based on health information. They will not be interested in your business and its achievements unless it in some way directly benefits them, but they will want to know what you, as their local pharmacist, recommends for various minor ailments.

So pick a topic, possibly one that is particularly relevant to your area, research it thoroughly so you know the advice you are giving is accurate and up to date and then write an article about it. As mentioned use simple language with short sentences and interesting pictures.

Try to link the information with the offer you are making in the accompanying letter and encourage the clients to come into your shop for more information, to purchase something or to use one of your services. The response will not be immediate but it will work over time. This will create a relationship between you and your clients.

## Always Have Good Headlines

Create an attention grabbing headline. This is the short sentence at the head of your page before the salutation. Generally once your clients have opened the envelope, you will have between 3 and 5 seconds to get them interested enough to actually read the letter you have spent hours crafting.

So it has to be good. Make it about the customer not you so rather than saying "we have this amazing offer" change it to "you can try this amazing offer". There are numerous books that will go into great length about headlines, their importance and give examples of ones that have made a lot of money for their authors.

Try to find a book by one of the best copy writers and then adapt them to something you are selling rather than starting from scratch which can be a bit daunting. We have used various headlines over the years though we find it difficult to pinpoint which work as we are more into relationship selling.

## Take Care How You Write Your Copy

Make the copy as interesting as possible. Copy is the rest of the letter after the headline. In it you will describe the features of your product and then explain the benefits this will give the client. As before you will use simple language in short sentences and paragraphs that can be easily understood.

Words are exceptionally powerful and can produce the most amazing results if used in certain ways. Research has shown changing the way something is written can make a huge difference to the way people react. For more information about this read a book called Yes by Noah J Goldstein, Steve Martin and Robert Cialdini.

There are two schools of thought—you can make it quick and easy to read so busy people can get the gist of the letter and make a decision there and then or make the copy longer and more detailed to give extra information about the benefits to the client. This is the sort of thing you could test to see what your customers prefer. Never make a decision for them. Let the market decide.

At the end of the letter have a call to action—that is tell them what you want them to do next i.e. fill in the coupon, give us a call, visit the website etc. This encourages them to take the next step.

## Use Images Frequently and Appropriately

Include pictures in your marketing where you can. A picture paints a thousand words and it can certainly attract attention. The image most likely to capture your readers interest is that of the human form, especially the face and even more so if it is a baby or a beautiful women.

You will have noticed how shower gel, shampoo, soap etc. often show women in the shower, while cars frequently have beautiful girls driving or riding in them. The message is that if you buy our product you will become a beautiful person and we all know it's not true but it still attracts attention.

So see how you can relate a picture to what you are selling. Always remember to put a caption under every picture. Your clients may not have worked out the message you are trying to convey so make it simple for them. The picture should be at the top of the page because it is what your clients will look at first. Their eyes will then travel down the page so anything above the picture will be missed. The most common mistake is to put the headline above the picture where it will lose it's impact.

## Make Your Mailing Relevant

Ensure the product or service you are writing about is relevant to your audience. There is little point writing about or making offers on say head lice treatment in the middle of the school holidays or trying to sell antihistamine tablets in the middle of winter. Similarly if the majority of your customers are under 45 marketing incontinence pads will not produce a lot of business whilst marketing nappies to an elderly population is not a great idea.

Also think about their income range. Marketing expensive items to cash-strapped young parents is not going to do too well, though they will spend a lot of money on their children at Christmas. However young professionals and older couples whose children have left home will have spare cash to spend on luxuries. So you need to know your customers, their interests and income brackets.

# Always Test Your Direct Mail

Don't assume that the headline, offer or price you have chosen to send out is the best it can be. You should test every aspect of your mailing to see if it can be improved. You only test one thing at a time. So if you decide to try two different headlines, you would keep every other part of the mail out the same, including the day and time you post. This way the only difference is the headline.

"The Best Solution to Your Problem
for Only £9.99"
or
"The Best Solution to Your Problem
for Only £29.99"

Send half with the original headline and the other half with a new headline. Then by counting the number of sales or enquiries you get from each headline you can see which one gives you a greater response. Very often the difference will not be significant but occasionally you will discover a headline that gives a much better result. This one then becomes your standard headline which you test against everything else.

You repeat this process with each part of the mailing till it is producing the best sales it can. Do remember that time changes and eventually the product or the offer will have to change but use it until that time comes.

## What Can You Send?

The most common way is to send a letter in an envelope, but you can choose A4, folded A4 or trifold A4; white or coloured envelopes. You can send a letter, flyer, catalogue, booklet, pamphlets etc. You could use a postcard.

Another option would be "bulky mail". One thing you could do is send a high quality wrapped teabag, with the message "Make yourself a cup of tea on us, relax and enjoy the rest of this letter".

If you were a garage you could send a wrapped model of a car and ask the client to consider the features and benefits of a car you are trying to sell. The advantage of this is that it is unlikely that the model of the car will be thrown away quickly. It might even be passed on to another potential client. This is an expensive mailing but there is a huge profit if you sell a car.

# Why?

From our experience this is one of the most cost effective ways of marketing your business. An offer letter will cost you about 70p to send and can cover as many clients as you want. It is like having a whole extra workforce talking to your clients all the time.

This is especially true as the use of email becomes more and more common. Fewer and fewer businesses are sending stuff through the post which means your information will stand out more, particularly if it has a normal postage stamp rather than being franked.

By sending out letters about offers and services on a regular basis you will be the first pharmacy that comes to mind (TOMA) when your customers need some help. If you include educational material you will be seen as the local health expert and also be fulfilling part of your public health role from the contract.

Finally by making various offers, your customers will be attracted to your pharmacy on a regular basis in the hope of getting a bargain.

LYNDA CHANIN

# Chapter Four: Internet

"One of the Internet's strengths is its ability to help consumers find the right needle in a digital haystack of data."
—Jared Lawrence Sandberg
(former Major League Baseball third baseman for the Tampa Bay "Devil Rays")

## 1. Search Engine Optimisation (SEO)

The design of your website is very important, but before that you need to consider the name you attach to your website. There are billions and billions of websites with the numbers growing all the time. People are overloaded with options when they input a search phrase into Google. The main site can also be linked to as many other domain names as you want.

Domain names are unique website identifiers and can be redirected to your main site, or to a page within your main site. If you want to check the availability of a domain name go to www.easy-space.com. And search for names which you could use.

Research has shown that generally only those websites quoted on the first page of Google actually get looked at. So it is important that you try to get on that front page. That can only be done three ways: you either pay for advertising, pay for somebody to position your site or your site becomes so popular that it rises to the top.

Paying for advertising can be very expensive. The usual rate is £10 to £15 per click if the ad is at the top of the page or about £1 to £2 if it is at the side. Of course just because somebody clicks on the advert does not mean they will buy from you. In fact some people just click on them knowing that you will be charged each time they do.

So paying for an expert to position your site is a much more reliable option, but that will cost £1000s of pounds as it takes a lot of time and effort. You also have to ensure you are choosing somebody who understands the changing dynamics of the web. The best list position used to rely on "metatags" that the search engines would recognise to improve your listing, but nowadays Facebook, Twitter and recommendation from other sites have changed all that.

By finding out what your clients would put into the search engine to find your service and then naming your website using those words will help them put you on the first page at no extra cost to you.

Many organisations promise to put you on the first page of Google but they then use search words that none of your prospective clients would use. It is IMPERATIVE that you choose the word or phrase that YOUR prospects or clients would put in to locate you. It is no good using the phrase "Solidwater limited," when all your clients know the pharmacy as "Ellis Road Pharmacy". A good SEO (Search Engine Optimisation) will be able to search google and work out what your potential customers would look for.

## 2. Naming Your Website

So if you think your best seller could be a particular product e.g. Blood pressure machines you could set up a domain called bloodpressuremachines.com which then links into your main site. Now the chances are that that name has long gone (at the time of writing bloodpres-suremachines.com is taken but .co.uk is available for £9.98 for two years), but you get the idea.

The extension is important. Google will recognise .com, .co.uk and .org and a few others as top level ones. So it is bet-ter to have an unusual combination of re-lated words with a .com extension then an obvious one with a less well known extension.

For pharmacy businesses it is important to add your location as a metatag and use it in the copy of your website, be-cause your customers may well put in to the search engine something like "phar-macies in the Bath area" when they are looking for some information.

# 3. Links Can Help Your SEO

Links are high speed connections from your website to other websites. They make it easy for your clients to find more information on anything that catches their eyes. So it is a good idea to have a number of links that are helpful to your clients. Furthermore as one of the contract requirements is that you signpost your patients to other health and social care professionals who could help them with whatever their problem is, these links would help you do this.

One of the problems of linking to other sites is that once your clients have followed that link they are no longer on your site. So it is a good idea before they leave your site, to explain to your visitors that to return to your site they should press the "back" button on the browser when they are ready. Be careful not to have sites that compete with your products and services either linking to or advertising on your site. You don't want your clients spending their time and money with your competitors.

The position of your website on Google will be influenced partly by the number of links that you have coming in to your website. This gives an indication to Google as to how popular your site is, which in turn will increase it's ranking i.e. put it closer to the first page.

## 4. Are People Coming to Your Site?

So how do you know if people are visiting your site? The only way you can do that is by using a company that will count the number of people who go to your site. They will tell you how many pages were visited each day, how many unique visitors you had and how many return visits. These companies will also provide you with the most popular searches your customers used to find you, the pages they visited the most, where they came from and where they moved on to. They charge about £5 per month for as many websites as you have up and running and you can use them as often as you wish.

## 5. How Will I Encourage Clients to Visit?

You must market your website and the best way is through the normal marketing channels i.e. on all communications with clients or prospects, on your labels, prescription bags, window, delivery vehicle, etc. You will notice that the BBC always direct viewers to their websites for further details about the programme you have just been watching. This ensures a constant stream of visitors. At the end of every email you write, put a link to your website.

However like the shop, you have to have a really interesting site once they get there or they will not bother to come back. So keep in mind that people are only looking for information, discounts or something funny/interesting to show to friends. How does your website stand up to those criteria?

# 6. Data Capture

As you design your website, think very carefully about the front page. What exactly do you want your visitors to do when they come to your site i.e. what is your most wanted action? It has to be all about them, not about you and your company. As with all advertising nobody is interested in you or your products only in the ways it can make their lives better, cheaper, more successful etc.

However just getting people to visit your website is not good enough. If they do not leave their details you cannot continue a dialogue with them that will eventually lead to a sale. You need to encourage them to give you their information. At the very least a name and address and prefer-ably an email and telephone number.

So how do you encourage that? Well the obvious answer is a free gift and the best one of those is a tips booklet about a subject they would be interested in. Luckily with your niche market there are 100s of topics you could choose from. A tip booklet is ideal from a number of reasons:

- It is a free gift and, in the universal tradition of reciprocity (if somebody gives you something you have to give something in return), it will make them more inclined to buy from you.

- As it will be downloadable, it will cost you nothing, after the initial work to create it.

- It will increase your standing in the community as an expert.

Most people read the front page of a website in a Z shape so you want your headline to start at the top left and the box with the information you want to col-lect, should be on the bottom right—all above the fold. This means the customer should not have to scroll down to see anything important. It is here you put your video (see p.58). The best place is probably opposite the data capture form. Research has shown the best colour for a data capture form is green.

# 7. Vouchers

Another good way to encourage your visitors to return to your site is to produce vouchers that they can print off and then bring into your bricks and mortar shops to receive discounts. These can be designed to suit your business. If you have a particularly slow day in the week e.g. on a Tuesday, you may entice more clients with a 10% off only on a Tuesday, etc. It's a good idea to change your vouchers on a regular basis much like your window display, as this will keep your clients returning to see what vouchers you have there this week.

On the other hand you may target a particular age group e.g. money-off coupons for young Mums or elderly people or off a particular product. Make sure you have a way of tracking these purchases e.g. put a code on them so they can be linked to a certain day.

# 8. Twitter

These days to achieve a high ranking on Google, which is the lead search engine, you have to engage with your visitors as much as possible and this is where twitter comes in. Twitter is a site which you sign up to and then make statements that are no more than 140 characters long. It is a snap shot of your life.

The idea is that you have followers who sign up to your twitter and are therefore notified of anything that you post. Many famous people use twitter to keep in contact with their fans. As an individual you may think it is a pointless exercise, only really intended for those interested in celebrity culture.

However, as a business it's a way to become "viral" i.e. that many customers are following you that your ranking in Google rises, hopefully to the top of that elusive first page. So once you set up your Twitter account you have to advertise on all your usual marketing material with the Twitter symbol that is universally recognised.

# 8. Facebook

Facebook has become a phenomenon in the last few years and most people now have their own Facebook page where they interact with the friends and family. Each individual has a short profile about themselves and then invites people to join them or accepts offers to become other peoples friends. You can put videos and photographs on line that you think other people will like especially if they are funny or have a point to make.

It is called social networking and is used in a variety of ways. It can be used by friends and family to keep up with one another, especially if they don't see each other regularly, it can be used by parents (and even employers) to keep an eye on what their children (employees) are up to and much more worrying it can be used by bullies to intimidate their victims and stalkers to groom young children.

However as a business it can keep your clients informed of what your pharmacy is doing, events you are running, successes you have achieved, campaigns you would like them to join in. Again like

Twitter you place the Facebook symbol on all your usual marketing materials to let people know you are on Facebook.

# 9. Video

As I have explained before with billions of websites to choose from people will stay on your site for just a few seconds before they move on unless something interests them enough to linger. The research has shown that a short video is 400% more effective than no video. It shouldn't be more than 90 seconds long.

A "talking head" is a good idea as the human face is one of the best ways to attract attention. This is the same for almost any advertising media. So a video of you explaining the major benefits of your products and services should do the trick. If you are unsure of your ability to do this, there are many companies that can produce a short video for you at a fairly reasonable price.

This video can then lead the visitor to other longer videos giving more detailed advice on certain selected conditions which can then be linked to products you would recommend for that condition, preferably that they can then order from your site. This obviously involves you having a shop on your website which would cost you more.

# 10. Content

Now we come to content. Your website should not be about you and your company. It should be all about your clients and what you can do for them. People have no interest in your company other than how it can make their life easier by saving them time and energy.

The majority of people visiting the web are looking for information and/or ways to save time and money. So you may want to think how your website can reflect that. Bearing in mind yet again that your have a niche market, how much health information does your website provide?

Thus the front page, or landing page as it is often called, should reflect your concern for your customers welfare not about how great your company is or how long you have been in business or that you "pride yourself" on anything. Maybe the opening phrase should be along the lines "not feeling well" or "want some advice from somebody you trust."

Does it give your pharmacists' take on various treatments for common ailments? Your clients have come to trust your judgement and when they are not feeling well they would prefer to take the advice of somebody who has proved over the years that the advice they give is sound.

Remember the details for various conditions is available everywhere but only your website will have your recommendations for treatments.

# Chapter Five: TV and Radio Advertising

"The only purpose of an advert is to
sell product—not win awards."
—Jay Abraham, US Marketing Guru

"A good advertisement is one which
sells the product without drawing
attention to itself."
—David Mackenzie Ogilvy, CBE
(UK widely known as
"the father of advertising")

## 1. Why?

TV advertising brings the quickest response of any advertising medium. It is
possible to target your audience by
choosing the programme that the advert
will appear in as well as your area, if you
are not a national company. For pharmacy that would be health related programmes. There is now the possibility of
choosing one of the minor channels
which have smaller specialist audiences
and tend to be less expensive.

A couple of points you need to consider is ensuring you have enough stock of the item being advertised to fulfill the demand that will be created. It will be very counter productive if you have large numbers of clients ready to buy your product or service and it is not available.

With radio choosing where to advertise should be less of a problem as the only option is commercial radio but it is more targeted to areas, so if you only have a couple of local shops this might be the best idea. You personally may loath the repetitive messages on local commercial radio, but it is that very repetition that makes it so effective!

## 2. Why Not?

TV advertising is very expensive. Not only do you have to pay for the air time but also to create the advert. You need a script, actors, director, film crew etc. All of which costs money. It will be much more if you decided to go nationally and that is only needed if you have branches nationwide.

However there is one form of TV advertising that might be more cost effective and that is the selling channels like QVC. Here you can go on for short bursts to extol the virtue of your product/service and give a demonstration of how it works. The drawback to this is you may need large quantities of products or lots of time available to meet the demand. You may be left with product if the response is not as good as you had hoped.

On the whole for a small independent it is unlikely that TV will be a cost effective form of advertising. However local radio may create business for a lot less money. We remember what we hear five times longer than what we see so it should make more of an impact with your clients.

## 3. When Should You Air Your Ad?

You will need to do quite a lot of research to decide what the majority of your clients watch or listen to. You should be aware of the demographics of your clients—you can find this out from government statistics. Then you find out what the demographics of the various programmes on the radio/TV. This way you can match the programme and channel to your customers.

Look out for a book on radio/TV advertising that may give you some good tips
on who to approach at the station and
what they will be expecting from you in
the way of material. As with all advertising you will need an attention grabbing
headline that is away motivated. The
opening words are the headline and this
should sell the rest of the advertisement.

## 4. What It Takes to Make a
   ## Great TV/Radio Ad

Stew Birbower (a former Madison Avenue
Creative Director from the 1960s to the
1990s) claims that to make an ad successful you should:

1. Catch their attention,
2. Penetrate their mind, and
3. Warm their heart.

He also says "the right music is an essential ingredient". Just how you achieve
these factors is probably best left to professionals, which can be costly.

## 5. Script

When using radio or TV advertising the
script is very important because people
can understand words they hear five

times more than the average person can speak.

At normal speed a person will say about 125 words per minute but you can understand about 525 words a minute. This means that if you can get an announcer to speak really quickly you can get a lot of information in a radio or television advertisement and the listeners will still get your message.

Always have a call to action and repeat this so they have time to get a pen and paper to record the details.

## 6. Who?

Unless you are very confident it is unlikely that you will want to star in your own advert but there are many jobbing actors and presenters who will do a voice over for you. With the readily available technology these days you can probably get a professional video made for a reasonable cost.

Make sure you have a clear idea of what you want your message to be as advertisers may well get carried away with what they think will be a good idea. Again with many advertising agencies they may be more interested in winning awards than selling your products so keep them focused on the benefit to the client.

However this will still be a lot more than other forms of advertising so the products and services you are marketing must have a good profit margin. Obviously it will be more cost effective if you have several branches in a small area so they will all benefit.

## 7. How Often?

As with all advertising repetition is the key. The more you clients see or hear an advert the more they will remember but you don't have to do it all the time. Coke discovered that if they only advertised for short bursts people thought they were on the TV all the time.

So you can advertise maybe on a daily basis for a week once a month or on a weekly basis for three months once a year. You may find this is enough to raise your profile. The best way to decide what gives you the most sales is to keep records.

Again as with all adverts, if you can give the viewer or listener useful information and then advertise your pharmacy they will listen more and it will establish you as the expert in the field. Educational marketing is by far the best way to get results.

LYNDA CHANIN

# Chapter Six:
# Window Displays

"A successful window is one that clearly delivers a message directly to the client. Whether this be communicating a brand campaign or promoting a new product launch it is all about engaging with the customer passing and giving them an insight into the values and personality behind the brand and the products it sells."
—Stuart Henry, founder of JUST So (London Agency specialising in Visual communications)

## Window Displays are Free

Use your windows as an advertising space. There is generally a lot of concern that money is wasted when advertising. A window display in your pharmacy is essentially free! People pass your shop all the time so an attractive or intriguing window display can catch their attention, which is half the battle when it comes to advertising. It also shouts loud of a pharmacy that takes care of it's image.

Many pharmacies that have large windows put the back of gondolas in them, which is very unattractive. However, you can overcome this by covering the back of the gondolas with coloured silk that matches the length you are going to use on the window sill and acts as a back drop.

On the other hand some shop fitters put slat board on the gondola backs so you slot in small plastic shelves to hold the products you wish to display. You can still hang coloured silk over the back and then put the slats in place. By changing the silks regularly you will keep the interest up.

## Window Displays Say a Lot About Your Pharmacy

Think about the message you are trying to send to your clients. What your windows look like says a lot about your pharmacy. If you have grills covering them during the day it suggests that you consider the area to be rough and you are at risk. This may discourage people coming into your shop.

Your clients like to see where they are going, so if their view is obstructed say with the back of gondolas or lots of out-dated posters, they may be less inclined to come in. Keep any display you create low level so your clients can still see through the window into the shop. Make sure the shop is well lit to attract clients in.

## Keep Your Windows Clear

Remove unnecessary posters and signs. As you are part of the community, it is very tempting to put up local notices when you are asked but these clutter the valuable selling space of your window. What's more, unless someone is nominated to make sure these posters are regularly removed once the event has passed, you end up with lots of tatty, out of date, yellowed posters. If you feel it is important to have these notices, provide a board within the shop.

If you really have too much window display areas you could make some of them work for you by offering to rent them out to another local business that either hasn't got any window space or is not in such a heavily populated area. Make sure they keep their window displays fresh and varied so they don't tarnish your reputation.

# Keep Your Window Spotless

Get your windows cleaned inside and out on a regular basis. It is important to keep your windows clean. This is the first part of your pharmacy that your customers see. If it is dirty and full of dead flies it does not present a modern, professional, vibrant image. You may need to clean them in between the times the window cleaner comes if customers are sick on them or children put sticky fingers over them.

Also make sure they are maintained i.e. repaired and painted on a regular basis. A tatty window will put people off from coming in.

# Make an Offer

Make an offer in your window display but of course you must be sure you also make a profit. Ensure you have bought your stock at a good price so you can sell it at a reduced price and still make money. Look for bargains everywhere that will reflect the general offering your business makes.

Repeat the offer by the till so your team can point it out as the customers make their purchases. Explain to the staff that they will probably sell to just one or two clients in every 10 or they will get disheartened when several times their offer is turned down.

Make copies of your offer stock purchase invoices which you then refer back to calculate the profit you made and whether the offer is worth repeating.

## Make the Display Relevant

The theme you choose for your window display must be relevant. There is little point having a holiday display in the middle of October when the children are back at school. Far better then to have one about head lice treatments or how to lower the chances of catching a cold/flu.

Plan out the year's window displays so you have time to get the supporting props and offers in place and a chance to design an eye catching one, using ideas from magazines or other window displays in the large shopping centres.

# Change the Display Often (We Don't Sell flies!)

Change your window displays regularly and make them spotless each time. If you have the same offers for too long your customers will get used to the display and it just becomes part of the background noise of daily life. Also they begin to look tired and dusty, showing a lack of care in your business.

So change them preferably as often as weekly, but certainly monthly, to maintain your clients' interest. If you use the system in the next tip you will find your window can be changed in less than an hour. Nominate one member of staff to be in charge of window displays or if it is too much have two that swap on a monthly basis.

# Keep the Display Simple and Uncluttered

Make your displays simple with maybe three offers depending on the size of your window. Do not puts loads of stock in, as this will just confuse your clients. Do not use the back of make-up stands etc. to form the backdrop of your window. The general rule is groups of 3 or 5 of the products you are selling. It also means that the window can be changed much more quickly and easily.

You can always add a few props to make the windows look more attractive and re-inforce the theme of the window. There will probably be somebody on your team who is artistic and would enjoy creating interesting displays with hearts and flowers for Valentines or Mothers Day, etc. However make sure that you give them a set time or they may well disap-pear for the whole day!

## Give Your Window a Theme

Try to have a theme to your window, where possible. Mixing children's feeding bottles with pain killers just sends mixed messages so make sure all the products are linked in some way. It will create a more attractive display and your custom-ers will understand the subject more eas-ily. A leading brand will often signpost what the display is about e.g. a window display around holiday health may have a bottle of Ambre Solaire as a marker.

Link in props so the theme is even more obvious e.g. if you want to do something on osteoporosis having a skeleton would be eye catching and quickly point out what the theme of the window is.

## How to Create a Window Display

To create a simple, inexpensive display buy some plastic food storage boxes in a variety of sizes. Get some shiny plain lining material in a variety of colours from your local haberdashery. You will need about 1.5m which should not be expensive. Darker colours are better as a background but pale pink for Mothers Day and pale yellow to represent sand or spring are useful as well.

Arrange the boxes in the clean window, some being on top of others to produce a bit of height but not too much, lay your chosen material over them and then put your offer products in groups of 3 or 5. Have a plastic A3 display holder with a poster explaining the theme for the whole window and then several A4 stands stating the offer for each related product. This poster should feature the product with a small explanation of it's benefits (which you will usually find on the back of the item), the price and the amount your clients will save.

You can add some decorative or eye-catching props such as dried leaves in Autumn, small soft bunny rabbits or chicks at Easter, glitter and stars etc. at Christmas or even say an old bicycle just to raise curiosity in your passers by. The more interesting your windows the more likely your clients are to look, notice your great offers and come in to buy. More often than not.

## Clinically Themed Window Displays

You can also create effective window displays for services that you offer such as smoking cessation, blood pressure testing or Lipotrim. Here you set up the window display as before but instead of product you use the A4 posters to explain the service, the benefits and how to join the scheme.

You can also staple three of the relevant leaflets explaining the service together in a fan shape which can then be leant against an A5 or A4 plastic stand on one of the boxes to great effect. If the service you are advertising has some national support you may get some advertising material from the central office to help e.g. No Smoking Day etc. Obviously if there are relevant products available as well, include them in the window.

# Chapter Seven: Selling Skills

"Internalize the Golden Rule of sales that says: All things being equal, people will do business with, and refer business to, those people they know, like and trust."
—Bob Burg
(American author and speaker. Born 1958, Florida, USA)

"Sales are contingent upon the attitude of the salesman, not the attitude of the prospect."
—William Clement Stone
(American Businessman, 1902-2002)

## Acknowledgement

Acknowledge your customers as they enter the pharmacy with eye to eye contact and a smile. This makes them feel important and appreciated. This encourages them to stay even if you are busy with another client. Make sure neither you or your staff finish off chores or chatting before you move over to that client.

Another benefit for immediate acknow-
ledgement is that if the person coming in
is a would-be thief, then by showing
them that you have noticed them, they
will be less inclined to hang around to
steal.

## Greeting

Produce a script and train your team on
how you want your customers to be
greeted. We have already talked about
acknowledging everybody who comes
into your shop. Now you may want to
think about the actual greeting. My feeling is that in this country most people,
especially if they are older, appreciate
being called Mr., Mrs., Miss or Ms.... at
least at the start of a relationship.

So I would always train your staff to use
the patient's surname. I also feel that
"good morning or afternoon", rather
than "Hi ya", gives a more formal approach and this will help when creating
an authoritative attitude for providing
advice. If the patient has been waiting,
then rather than apologising for the
delay, always say "Thank you for being
patient". I cannot stress enough that
you should smile when greeting a client.
It may be the only smile they see all

day. It boosts everybody and builds on that positive attitude.

## Open Questions

Train your staff on the importance of open questions. An open question is one that cannot be answered by a short answer e.g. "How long have you been coughing?" is a closed question as the answer may be something like 3 days. An open question would be "Tell me about your cough?"

A better greeting than the commonly heard "Yes?" or "Are you OK there?" would be something like "How can I help you?" (easier to say than the more grammatically correct How May I help you?) because a fuller answer than "Yes" or "No" is required.

The more open questions they ask the more accurate picture they will have of the patient's problem. To give advice the staff must understand the condition. Also by listening actively i.e. concentrating on what is being said, they pick up vital clues as to the cause.

## Active Listening

It is common to use the time after you ask your first question to prepare to ask your second question. However, it is very important instead to listen carefully to what your customers are saying. Make sure your staff are trained on the 2WHAM system and use it constantly to gather as much information as they can about the patients' problem. The more fully they understand the better solution they can give. Also the patients will feel much more cared for if your team have shown real concern for them.

## Product Knowledge

Ensure your staff are fully trained on the products you sell. They should know what they are for, their main active in-gredients, what possible side effects they might have, who can and can't use them and suitable alternatives if the pa-tients don't like them. They should be es-pecially well versed in the products that your Pharmacist particularly likes. The phrase "This is one our pharmacist par-ticularly recommends" will go along way to closing the sale, and gaining a satis-fied customer.

Under the contract you are expected to train your staff on an ongoing basis. By running weekly quizzes to check their knowledge with prizes for the most accurate you will fulfil this requirement. An added benefit is the more you train your staff the more motivated they will be and the more likely to stay with you.

## Features and Benefits

Explain to the team the difference between the features of a product and the benefits. For example, the features of a medicine are things like

1. It contains paracetamol, or
2. Dissolves in half an hour.

These translate to benefits in that

1. Paracetamol will lower your temperature as well as easing your headache, so covering more of your symptoms
2. By dissolving in half an hour they will begin to work quickly, and you will be able to get back to what you want to be doing.

All the patients are interested in is, will it solve the problem they have, how quickly and how expensive it will be. For every feature of a product there will be a benefit and it is your team's job to explain all that to the patients. The more fully informed a patient is the more likely they will be to buy and will associate your pharmacy as the source of the best information.

However don't forget they have the right to make the wrong decisions in your eyes. If, despite all your suggestions, they choose to go with an old tried and tested favourite let them, so long as they will not come to harm. We have all had patients who ask for something for their cough, and after having explained which one is best for them they say "I'll just have the Benylin please". However the practice of Pharmacy is often something of an art, as well as a science, and their belief in that treatment may well be the key to them getting better.

## Appearance

Make sure both your pharmacy and team look neat and tidy. The better your pharmacy looks (and this extends to printed materials), the more confidence your clients will have in the services you provide. So have a good look at your premises. Are they bright, cheerful and inviting? Can your customers see into your shop as they approach? Is it easy to navigate around your pharmacy?

Are your staff presenting a neat, clean and tidy image? Do they keep their hair and nails clean and are well groomed? Have they lots of tattoos and piercings? This sort of thing can detract from the confidence patients have in your pharmacy.

Do they have uniforms that are well maintained? Have you asked your clients what sort of uniform they think the staff should wear? It might be an idea to run a survey with the same person wearing different outfits e.g. casual, smart uniform, white coat and see which one's advice they are more likely to follow.

## Positive Attitude

Think about the attitude you and your staff have towards life in general and especially towards your clients. The more positive the atmosphere in your pharmacy the more people will want to come in and be part of it. As the leader of your team, your staff will be influenced by the way you behave. So the more positive

you are the more positive they will be.
Then as your clients come into your
shop, this vibrant, welcoming ambiance
will encourage them to linger and to purchase more. This will build your profits.
So, if you arrive at work with a slight
hangover, having just argued with your
wife, you would be better thinking of the
first contact with your staff being a per-
formance. Think of the time you were
most happy and BE HAPPY and upbeat.

Never allow your staff to be rude to a client. If the customer is rude then teach
your staff to try to be understanding
about what has upset them and try to
overcome the problem. If you see your
staff at any time being rude, they should
be disciplined. This can do untold dam-
age to your business. A customer who re-
ceives bad service will tell, on average,
13 other people and for every complaint
you receive 16 other people will have felt
the same. If you bring a customer complaint around, so they are happy with
you it is extremely likely that they will
become an excellent advert for you.

## Upselling and Cross-Selling

Merchandise your products so linked
sales occur naturally. For example have

tissues and sanitising hand gel by the cough and cold remedies, as well as by the tissue section and with the creams. Teach the staff to bring these up in the selling sequence. Create a list of possible linked sales so the staff are aware of what they are most likely to sell together, e.g. Dentists advise that you should replace your toothbrush every three months, so put the toothbrushes near (or tape a toothbrush to some packs of toothpaste) the toothpastes.

Explain to the staff the benefits for the customer of making the linked sale e.g. if they are buying cold and cough remedies they will need to wipe their nose and disposable tissues are much better than handkerchiefs because they can be thrown away (feature) and so reduce the risk of re-infection (benefit) or sanitising hand gels are good because they can be used without water, (feature) so it can be used when you are out and about (benefit), again to help stop the spread of reinfection.

Always praise your staff when they make a linked sale. Also encourage them to sell the larger quantities where possible. In the case of medicines, there are times when a larger size does make sense. For example, if a mother has a family of four, a pack of 32 paracetamol, whose dose is up to 8 tablets per day per individual, is not going to last long, so be practical when selling. It is better that you provide all her needs rather than her having to stop at the local supermarket to get more. One benefit of the pharmacy is that we are legally allowed to sell up to 100 if needed.

## Types of Sales Staff

A study at Harvard University found that there are three kinds of sales people. (Those people assessed were all professional sales people). There are

1. Meeters and Greeters,
2. Negotiators and finally
3. Closers.

About 15% are meeters and greeters. These people love meeting people, especially for the first time, and find it easy to make people feel welcome. 85% are negotiators and will happily discuss features and benefits all day long and sometimes never close a sale. Finally 10% are closers, and they will ask the client if they want to buy the product, but the thought of meeting and greeting would be alien to them.

Over time sales people can learn to encompass all three sales types, which is when they become really good!

## The Seven Stages of Selling

Your counter staff are often called sales assistants, in which case their job is to assist in the sales. These steps are the most likely to achieve a sale.

Remember that only 3% of the general population will be looking RIGHT NOW for the product you are selling, which means that most people will not buy it. This is why sales staff need a positive mental attitude when customers reject the sale, and remember the refusal is for the product and not the sales assistant. However, a further 7% will wish to purchase AT SOME TIME in the future, and these are the people you can persuade.

For all those people who don't want to buy now, you need to create what is referred to as TOMA or Top of Mind Awareness. You need to carry on marketing to them so that you are the first pharmacy they think of when they need anything.

Hopefully, as your clients have taken the trouble to come into the pharmacy, more than 3% are ready to buy.

It is worth noting that only 13% of people in a recent study who came in specifically to collect a prescription ever buy any other products.

## Stage One: Establish Rapport

Studies show that 40% of the client's buying decision is made if they have excellent rapport with the sales person.

Rapport is present if the client LIKES you, TRUSTS you and RESPECTS you. In the retail situation it is best to employ attractive, confident and happy people who like people. If your assistants smile a lot and acknowledge clients as soon as they walk in, they will be seen as likeable. If your assistants are encouraged to treat your clients just as they would a close friend, clients will like them. This does not mean false flattery but real advice.

Trust is built when you never lie to a client, you never exaggerate or bluff, and you never over-promise and under-deliver. These qualities will also gain clients respect over time.

Respect can be built by educating the client about their condition etc.

## Stage Two: Find the Need

Studies show this accounts for a further 25% of the buying decision. This can only be done by asking questions. The more open ones you use the more information the client will tell you about what they really want.

## Stage Three: Build Value

This is the stage where you find the product that you feel would be most suitable for the client and then go on to explain why you think it is the one for them.

You describe the features of the product —imagine you were describing a medication that would ease their cough. You might say, this cough medicine has pholcodine in it.

Now that is a feature (something about the product) however the client is only interested in what it will do for her. So you would go on to explain that it will help stop her coughing. (Benefit)

Which means that she will sleep better at night or will be able to attend that lecture or concert they were invited to, without annoying everybody else by constantly coughing. (Positive outcome(s) following on from the benefit.)

Building the value also includes building the value of buying from you. For example, you might be a trusted pharmacy, having served the community for generations, etc.

## Stage Four: Create Desire

Here is where you tell the client why this is the product they should buy now. Maybe because you have a special offer on it or because it will make them feel better with no side effects.

You might also offer a money back guarantee if that is possible so you are taking the risk rather than them or tell them how other clients found it worked for them.

## Stage Five: Overcome Objections

Now if you have done your job correctly in the previous stages there should be no objections but if there is you must NOT try to argue.

You agree with the client, saying something along the lines of "I can quite see where you are coming from, pause, then but can I just ask...?"

And then you try to find out more detail about their objection and go back over the previous steps to reassure them. So maybe they will say the product is too much. You would ask "Is that your only objection?"

If they say "yes," then all you have to do is find a way to make it affordable, e.g. some way of paying a fixed amount over time—such as a credit account etc. or a smaller amount.

## Stage Six: Close the Sale

Closing a sale is something that is often missed in the selling cycle. It is a vital part of the process but is rarely taught. Studies on sales people have shown that as few as 10% are natural closers. If you want to improve your sales you need to teach your staff to get better at this.

Having listened carefully to the symptoms the patient has described, considered the possible treatments and decided on a suitable one, the staff member simply has to close the sale i.e. would you like that in cherry or blackcurrant flavour, would you like that wrapped, are you paying by credit card or cash etc.

Listen to your staff during the day. Do they remember to close the sales or is this an area that needs attention?

**Stage Seven: Follow Up**

Again this is an area that is sorely neglected. I have seen descriptions of the sales cycle where this section is not even included.

And yet it is probably the most important step of all. This is the step that keeps your clients returning to you. How many times have you employed somebody to do some work on your house and were so impressed with their work that when you want something else doing you would like to re-employ them. If that person has kept in touch with you, sent you useful information about the service they provide, then you would automatically re-employ them for the next stage of the work you needed done.

However in the meantime you have lost their details and can't remember their name so you can't look them up on the internet. So you just start the cycle of choosing a new person all over again.

The most important people to your business are your clients, and you must follow up any contact you have with them. In your pharmacy, a lot of this will be done face to face each time they visit you.

This will require your staff to get to know them and to ask how the medication they recommended worked etc. But you will also need to follow up things like MURs, NMS, and MAS.

This will kill two birds with one stone as the commissioners would like to see evidence based results for these services. They want to see that you are saving the NHS money in the long term.

But follow up is more general, as we have mentioned before. So you should be sending personalised letters/or emails on at least a monthly basis with some useful information and your latest offer, some vouchers or details of an event you are holding. A regular newsletter on different healthy topics is always a good idea.

# Chapter Eight: Events

Three things a woman
LOVES to hear:
"I Love you."
"There's a Make-up
event at the Chemist."
"Spend as much as you want."
—Anon.

## 1. Investigate

Once you have decided to organise an event, you need to think about what you are trying to achieve. Is it simply to raise awareness of the issue, to raise money for a charity, improve your business etc. It may even be a combination of all 3. The next step is how are you going to measure the outcome?

If it is awareness of the issue you need to get the message out to as many people as possible so you would want to publicise it through the newspapers, on local radio and maybe even on the local TV. If it is to raise money, you may need to set a target and see how close you get, or if it's to improve the business see how much difference it makes to your turnover.

There are always hidden benefits to these sorts of events, in that it will enthuse your staff especially if they have some say in what event is chosen and how the money raised is spent etc. A motivated team is a great asset. Staff will pass that enthusiasm onto the clients they serve and there will be a lower turnover of staff. The whole atmosphere of the pharmacy will brighten.

## 2. Choose Site, Date, and Period

Having decided on the event you want to get involved in, you need to think about the date, the place and the props you might need. It is a good idea to do this several months before the time to allow for getting props together and organising publicity. If it is a set date, i.e. No Smoking Day, the times will already be chosen by the main organisers. This ties you down but on the plus side the central organisers will have many preprepared props that you can get. They may charge for this, which you will need to include in your costings.

How long you run the event is another decision. You may just do it for the actual day, the week or maybe even the whole month. The period chosen will influence how many props you will need and how much you want to raise. Be careful of running too many charity events in your pharmacy or your clients will get fed up with donating.

## 3. Organise

To make a success of any of these projects you need organisation. If this is not your strong point delegate it to somebody else but keep involved or it may just fizzle out. For each event have a folder both on your computer and in reality. In that make a note of the title, the date and the period the event will run for, where it is to be held and the aim.

Make a list of all the props you are going to need i.e. using the Fruity Friday theme T-shirts, fruit and fruit bowls, charity tins, window display material etc. Also list where you are getting them from with contact details and when. Then record who is going to be in charge of what and possibly when they will need to have finished various steps.

Refer back to the folders on a regular basis to ensure all is moving along as intended and record the progress. If problems do occur then make a note of what happened and how you over came them. This should create a manual if you need to trouble shoot next time.

## 4. Cost

It is important to keep on top of the costs that you incur. You may have decided that you are doing this as part of your public health requirements and therefore are prepared to run the idea at a loss but this is not something I would recommend. The whole point of you being in business rather than working as a locum or manager is to make a profit from which the government gets money through taxes.

So keep a detailed account of all the money you have spent and on what. Research where you can to get props as cheaply as possible. Consider what products and services you provide that could benefit from the promotion and train the staff to link those to the promotion. You may have to teach them what to say to begin with, as it is always difficult to know how to start a conversation.

As they become confident they will be able to use their own words.

Then keep a close eye on how much the promotions have benefited your business. How much has your turnover increased, how many more consultations have you done compared to a similar period last year. Finally decide was it cost effective? If not how can you tweak it so it will be?

# 5. Advertise

For an event to be a success it must be advertised in the same way your pharmacy is. This should start well in advance of the date so attendees can plan. It also gives you time to organise any sponsors or celebrities you may want to get involved.

The advertising should continue on a regular basis to keep it at the forefront of everybody's mind and an extra push as the date draws closer. Put posters in your windows and as many local shops, pubs, clubs etc. you can persuade to take them. Have flyers in the same places and also as an insert in the local papers. Give them out to all of your clients and the surrounding businesses.

Get a slot on local radio either as an advert or an interview, especially if it is a charity event or something around improving people's health. Repeat as often as you can. When a person hears something it lasts five times longer in the brain than when they see it so repetition is important.

## 6. Result

As with all the other types of advertising it is important to keep records, especially of the results. Was it successful? Did it create business, raise money, raise your profile in the community?

Again use the results for some PR with your local papers, magazines, local radio. Take pictures and write some editorial so the information is all there. Take pictures of the clients that joined in and make sure you make a note of their names and how they are spelt so they are accurate when they appear in the article.

This will ensure that at least some people in the local community will read the articles, as everybody loves to see themselves in print.

# 7. Topic

Events can be a way of making your pharmacy look fun and innovative. There are all sorts of ways to achieve this. You can have special days to celebrate something on the calendar. When it comes to health events the best place to look is on the Equip part of the NHS website.

So for example you could celebrate Fruity Friday in May, which is to encourage everybody to eat 5 portions of fruit and vegetable a day. It also helps raise money for cancer research. So the staff could dress up as pieces of fruit or wear tee shirts with the message across their chests. You could have a window display giving details of what constitutes a portion of various types of fruit and veg and sell fruit for 10p a portion with the money going to cancer research.

You could do the same thing around No Smoking Day to encourage patients to join your smoking cessation programme which would increase your turnover and profit or work on Sun Awareness week encouraging people to take more care in the sun which should help to boost your sales of suntan lotions. The list is endless.

# Chapter Nine: Telephone Sales

"If people like you they'll LISTEN to you but if they TRUST you they'll DO BUSINESS with you."
—Hilary Hinton "Zig" Ziglar
(American author, salesman and motivational speaker, 1926-2012)

## 1. Why?

Telesales is one of the most effective ways of creating a relationship with your clients, especially if they are house-bound. We have found it to be of great benefit when we were building up our business. However it does involve quite a lot of time and effort for it to be successful.

The simplest system is to send out an advertising piece in the mail or by email and follow it up with a phone call with your staff saying something along the lines- "We sent you out some information. I don't suppose you have had a chance to read it yet?" If they reply "yes" then you start discussing it with them. If they say "no" then you say "Well I'll just quickly go over the details with you".

The important thing is to remember that you want to create a relationship with your clients, so the more you can find out about them the more you can help them. Hence make sure your staff ask lots of open questions and have a customer relationship management system (CRM) in place where you can record all the details you learn.

## 2. What?

What you decide to market will depend on your clients once again but it is better with a product that has a good profit margin as this is a costly form of marketing. It is labour intensive and quite a skilled job if it is done properly so look at higher priced item like Blood Pressure machines, mobility products or some of the services.

Once again your sales team must know the product thoroughly and understand it's benefits as well as it's features so they can explain them to the client. It is also a good idea that they should be able to indicate why your pharmacy is better than your competitors e.g. if your main competition is a surgery pharmacy they could explain that because you are less busy you have time to get to know your customers.

## 3. Who?

It is important that the right person is chosen for this job. Ideally they should have a sunny disposition and like chatting to people. They also need to be confident as they will get a lot of rejections from people who are not interested in what they have to offer. However repetition is the key. Only 3% of people will be interested in buying what you sell at any one time. So you just have to keep your name in their minds until they are ready to buy again.

Now as to who you target, the person most likely to buy is the person who has just bought so your clients are the most likely to be interested in your new service/product. On the other hand you also need to contact those who haven't bought from you before as you always need new people to convert into clients.

As you learn more about your clients and put this information on your database you will be able to start targeting your advertising to those who are most likely to be interested i.e. MURs will be for the older person on more medication while a chlamydia scheme is obviously better aimed at the 18-24 year olds.

# 4. How?

When you have sent a mail out, the more people you can follow up with a phone call the more chance you will have of making a sale. So the number you mail or email should be kept roughly to the number you feel you will be able to phone in the few days following the posting. If you leave it much longer than that the interest will die down.

For example if you sent out a letter about your MURs or NMS services, you need to think about how many you could manage to run in the pharmacy. Say you were aiming for 10 a week MURs and 20 a week of NMS then you need to phone about 10 times that number i.e. 300 people. Make records of the conversations you have and any interesting points you discover during your chats. Even if you don't manage to persuade them to have an MUR/ NMS the first time, with persistence and regularly contact you may persuade them another time.

# 5. Script

As mentioned previously it is important the telesales staff have a script. This should involve an agreed form of greeting, a way of introducing themselves, a description of the product or service they are trying to sell, concentrating as always on the benefits to the clients rather than the features and a simple close.

They should know the product or service they are talking about well, so that they can answer any questions that might come up in the conversation. They need to have a check list before they start phoning—something along the lines of:

- Know what you are selling.
- Know your client or read your notes.
- Think positively.
- Smile.

The last point is important because your clients will be able to hear the smile over the phone and people buy from people they like so this is all part of building up that friendly relationship.

# 6. Incentives

Make sure you have a good incentive to reward your marketing consultants. It takes a certain type of person to do this job and they will respond to the challenge of a good reward. It doesn't always have to be money. Some people would prefer time off, whilst others may like recognition and will appreciate being employee of the month.

Run competitions, again with small rewards, to check they understand the products you sell and the benefits they provide to your clients. Maintain records of the number of clients phoned and the number they got through to, as well as the number they actually booked on to an MUR/NMS etc.

# Chapter Ten: Public Relations

"The only thing worse than being talked about is not being talked about."
—Oscar Wilde
(Irish writer Oscar Fingal O'Flahertie Wills Wilde, 1854–1900)

Question: "What's the difference between a Rat and a Squirrel?"
Answer: "PR".

## Support Local Health Campaigns

Find out what National or local health campaigns are being run in your area either by your LAT (or it's replacement) or local health authority. Investigate what you can do to support them. Research the topic that has been chosen and see how you could tie in a window display, especially if it means promoting some of your products and services.

Organise an event around the topic and invite the local newspaper to report it.

Write a short article about the campaign, what it means to the local community and how you want to help with pictures if possible. Then give this to the reporter or send it direct to the newspaper if a reporter cannot attend, so the newspaper understands the aim of the project and will have accurate information without having to search for it.

## Run Competitions

Organise competitions for interesting prizes. Try to get a local celebrity , the mayor or the local MP to judge the competition. This is more likely to encourage the local newspaper to want to report the event. Choose a health related basis for the competition e.g. running a painting competition to advertise your stop smoking service jointly with your local primary school. The prize could be some equipment the school wants e.g. a new computer.

You can get a reasonably good computer for about £350, which is probably less than you would pay for a small advert in the paper and will produce far more benefit for the school. It may also encourage parents to come into your shop as a supporter of their school.

Once the winner is announced, write to them congratulating them on their win but also write to everybody else who entered, explaining that you were sorry they didn't win but offering a consolation prize of a voucher say for 10% off any goods in store. This way you will increase the traffic in your store and have a reason to keep in contact with your clients. Take a photograph of the winner and include it in your emails.

## Talk to Your GP or Local Authority

Talk to your local authority and GPs regularly. Find out what plans they have and what they need help with. Go to all meetings that the local health organisations in your area invite you to. The more your face is seen at meetings the more you will be recognised and hopefully eventually asked to participate in planning the various health initiatives.

People with ideas are always welcome. So think of things that you feel could impact the local community with little cost implications. Talk to your clients. Very often the patients on the ground are the ones that have the greatest insight into the problems and possible solutions.

## Support National Health Campaigns

Be aware of the national health campaigns that are running. As part of the contract you are expected to participate in a maximum of 6 public health campaigns a year where you will be supplied with leaflets. By creating a window display, training your staff on the information, and encouraging them to chat with your clients you will help to improve the health of your neighbourhood. The powers that be, will also be impressed by your involvement which could stand you in good stead when they are commissioning services in the future.

## Write a Newspaper Article

Local newspapers are always looking for content that would interest their readers. This is an ideal opportunity to market your pharmacy through articles about health issues locally, nationally and internationally.

You could for example discuss the need to visit pharmacies as an alternative to a 2-3 day wait to see their GP or sitting in A&E for four hours or the importance of not taking antibiotics for viral infections, or your views on the local hospital closing etc.

Most newspapers will only want an article of about 200 words with possibly a picture plus caption and a snappy headline. As always you want to write using simple words, short sentences and paragraphs.

The paper will want to make sure that if they start a regular feature you will be able to keep it up, long term. So it would be a good idea to send them several articles to show that you will be reliable.

Over time they may start contacting you for your views on other health topics that come up in the news.

## Attend Local Events

Most communities have various health events or even just things like a festival where the local traders will display their goods and services. See if you can join in. Obviously you won't be able to sell a lot of medicines but you could certainly give advice and possibly perform some old dispensing functions like making creams just to create interest.

Think what products and services you want to increase awareness of and have offers on these. Choose the staff that man these stalls carefully. You are looking for the ones that like people and will be enthusiastic so will go up to visitors and invite them to try whatever you have on display.

## Celebrate

Have celebrations for new openings, services, birthdays etc. So if you have been in business for 25 years make a bit of splash. Invite your best customers to a special evening where they can have a glass of wine, a few nibbles and maybe a little fashion show tying in with your local boutique and showing off your make up ranges.

Or tie in the new service of vascular screening with a local sports team who want to promote their successes and future ticket sales. There are many ways you can promote your business in collaboration with another group. You just have to have some imagination and a little local knowledge.

Of course the most important aspect to this is to make sure it is well publicised through your local newspaper, radio station and nowadays your website.

## Support Newspaper Campaigns

Read through your local papers and listen to your local radio station looking for any projects they are supporting particularly if they are health related. Having selected one, think about how you can tie in with that project either by raising money or allowing some of your staff to take paid time off work to help in some way.

Advertise the project through your website, window displays, with leaflets and talking to your clients. Keep notes of what you do and the successes you have. Regularly update the newspaper or radio station so they can follow your progress as well. Have a board in your pharmacy with pictures and notes on, so your clients can see you commitment to their community.

## What is PR?

Using PR can be a powerful way to promote your business and if done well can be relatively cheap. Understanding the needs of your local media will help so try to get to know them. Find out what sort of information they like to put in their papers and what help they may need in various projects they are supporting. With regular contact you may become someone they approach for health information when needed e.g. during a pandemic etc.

Consider events you could attend to support the local community and even events you could organise e.g. having a summer party where all the local shops contribute to bring everybody together. When you do something along those lines make sure you keep records and photographs of what you did, how successful it was and any problems you had. This will make it easier to organise next time and means you can create displays in your shop of what you have achieved.

## How to Write a Press Release

We have gathered some good advice from people who regularly use press releases sent to them, including advice on how to get your press release noticed.

Before you write the release:

If the PR in question has time, have a quick look at the site they are pitching to, to get an idea of the tone of writing and the type of article that does well. Use this to make the press release a bit more relevant. (Rebecca Thomson, reporter, Computer Weekly)

Provide clear relevance to my 'beat'. I hate it when I am the recipient of scattered buckshot that has no relevance for my publication but I have to plough through a lot of information before I realise this. (Gillian McAinsh, La Femme editor, The Herald, South Africa)

Ask yourself these three questions:

1. Is your press release really necessary?
2. If you were running a story based on this release, what would be the headline be and does the first sentence fit into less than 15 words? If no, or the first sentence is "Mrs Miggins plc announces...", go back to Q1.
3. If you got Q2 right, why are you changing the wording for a press release? (Chris Edwards, freelance journalist)

## Format

Don't send the release as attachment only. A release under the phrase "Press release, see attached" and no other details is likely to be deleted with extreme prejudice and the company added to a spam list. (Mark Robertson, journalist/-producer, BBC Cumbria)

Send a pretty PDF of the release to your client if you must, but send copy to journalists as plain text. PDFs and other formats often add weird character breaks and slow down the editing process. (Carlton Reid, editor of bikebiz.-com)

## Headlines

Headlines should be as short and interesting as possible. (Rebecca Thomson, reporter, Computer Weekly, UK)

A headline should be short enough for a Twitter update including a link. (Sarah Taylor, Inspiring Communication)

If you're emailing the press release, you've only got a handful of words in the subject line to grab journalists' attention and if the first four are 'Press release:

Market leading...' chances are you're not going to get many hacks to actually read the rest of the subject line, let alone open the email/release itself. (Journalism.co.uk blog commenter 'Hack')

The headline should clearly contain the value of the press release to the reader. It should not contain the name of the issuing organisation—for example: "NPR announces new special initiative"—obviously it's NPR, they're sending the press release. (Matt Forsythe, social media manager, National Film Board of Canada)

## Subject Matter and Language

I get loads of press releases that are boring and paragraphs or even sentences containing lots of technical terms make me want to break things. Reporters get told to constantly ask the question when thinking of stories, "why would people care about this?" I think PRs should ask themselves that question when writing releases. (Rebecca Thomson, reporter, Computer Weekly, UK)

Press release writers should make it clear why my readers need to know about their product. That is, provide a news angle to their releases. (Gillian

McAinsh, La Femme editor, The Herald, South Africa)

The biggest bugbear with press releases I find is the vague, nonsensical terms—leading, highly scalable, holistic, end to end solution etc. Please, tell us in as plain a language as you can, what your client and their product does. (Journalism.co.uk blog commenter 'Hack')

My personal peeve is when press releases make tenuous, unbelievable tie-ins to current topics to get attention. Bad form. (Phill Dolby, freelance journalist)

Purge superlatives. (Carlton Reid, editor of Bikebiz.com)

**Summaries**

Bullet points at the top, summarising the main points, are helpful. (Rebecca Thomson, reporter, Computer Weekly, UK)

If you have to distribute a release that has already been approved by a client, try rewriting the first paragraph as a "news in brief" item and put that in the email before the press release. If you can condense your story into a NIB and save journalists some time, then it's more likely to be used. (Journalism.co.uk blog commenter 'Josie', referencing advice from social media consultant Nick Booth)

Summaries of the organisation's history or relevance are not required. A single line to tell us who you are is enough. (Matt Forsythe, social media manager, National Film Board of Canada)

## Paragraph structure

Summarise what you are selling early on in the release, preferably using the standard journalism 25 words of "who, what, where, when, why". Releases often lack the time and place of an event, which can make all the difference. (Gillian McAinsh, La Femme editor, The Herald, South Africa)

Don't bury any "actually, the study doesn't really show what the title of this press release says it does" content down toward the bottom. (Journalism.co.uk blog reader 'Anna')

Once you've written your press release, go away and make a coffee. Come back and notice that the whole point of the release is in the last paragraph. This is because you were thinking to A4 scale and after writing seven paragraphs of waffle you had a space of one-paragraph left in which to squeeze your essential. Now make the last paragraph your introduction and go and have a second well-deserved coffee. It's a cliché, but the sting is often in the tail. (Tony Trainor, freelance journalist)

## Length

Never, ever, write more than two pages —preferably one. (Sarah Taylor, Inspiring Communication)

Two-hundred-and-fifty words is enough to say everything. Add a link to a longer post if there are specific details that need to be added. (Matt Forsythe, social media manager, National Film Board of Canada)

## Quotes

Only include a quote that someone might actually have said. No "strategic partnership solutions" language (anywhere, but particularly not in the quote). (Sarah Taylor, Inspiring Communication)

Please don't quote people who aren't available for interview—there's nothing more annoying than getting a release and then finding the subject isn't available to talk. (Journalism.co.uk blog reader 'Hack')

## Case studies

Please stop sending me case studies. I don't care what Wigan Council has done with its IT support, unless it's moved its server to the moon or something. (Rebecca Thomson, reporter, Computer Weekly, UK)

## Images

Some differing opinions from our participants about the best way to handle images:

Fancy graphics or big pictures just fill up my inbox, meaning I might have to delete the release without really reading it. If I want pictures I'll ask for them, and graphics might look nice but they're just annoying to someone who gets hundreds of (uninteresting) emails each day. The release needs to be really easy to scan quickly and graphics can get in the way. (Rebecca Thomson, reporter, Computer Weekly, UK)

But if images are really an essential part of what your release is about:

Supply clear, usable photographs. (Gillian McAinsh, La Femme editor, The Herald, South Africa)

Always include two or three pictures in the actual release rather than fob people off to a website where they then have to spend ages finding images that you [the press release writer] should have found for them. (Journalism.co.uk blog reader 'Kate')

## Contact details

Don't send out a release and then go on holiday for two weeks the next day. It's amazing how often this happens. It's very annoying if you need to speak to the author urgently. (Journalism.co.uk blog reader 'Kate')

Always put your phone number somewhere instead of hiding behind an email address. There isn't always time for email queries. (Journalism.co.uk blog reader 'Kate')

# Chapter Eleven: Presentations

"There are 2 ways to share knowledge:
You can PUSH information out;
You can PULL in with a story."
—Anon.

## 1. Who to?

As mentioned previously there are any number of local community groups, Towns Women Guild (TWG), Women's Institute (WI), Rotary Club, Mother and Toddler Groups, Religious groups of various persuasions, schools, health groups based on one type of illness or another who meet to support each other.

You may want to consider targeting local businesses that employ predominately one type of worker that may have a specific health issue they would like information on. The list is endless once you start putting your mind to it.

So it is just a matter of deciding who you wish to target. What groups meet regularly in your community and when?

An evening meeting will be easier for you to attend. What problems are the major cause for concern both in the population in general and in your LAT/local authority?

Consider where that particular subject will have the most impact. A talk on how to reduce the chances of teenage pregnancy is going to be most effective if given to young girls at school whilst a discussion of the best way to have a good nights sleep may be more tailored to an older group like TWG.

## 2. Content

The content is very important. You should remember that the average reading age in this country is 8 years old and the most read paper is the Sun. So keep your talk simple and easy to understand. This is just as important when you are talking to an intelligent educated audience. The more complicated you make it the more bored they will become. Do not use long words or difficult explanations. Imagine you were telling a young relative about your topic.

Now, as you do when you are talking to youngsters, you have to be really enthusiastic about your subject. We have all listened absolutely enthralled by a TV presenter who tells us about the habits of some rare animal which we have no real interest in but his excitement is catching.

That is what you are aiming at. Know your subject and your talk on it by heart. Have pictures, tables, mindmaps etc. to illustrate the talk and brighten the proceedings. They will also help you to remember all you want to say. Do not make the slides too small or too crowded. They have to be able to be read from the back of the room.

## 3. Appearance

The more professional you appear the more weight is generally given to the information you provide. There has been quite a lot of research into people's response to authority. It has been shown that people are more likely to trust advice from a such a source.

So think carefully about what you are going to wear. Wearing a tee shirt and jeans, even though you may feel more comfortable may not be the best image to portray to your audience. You are representing not only your business but also the pharmacy profession and as such you should reflect that.

Personally I prefer to wear a smart trouser suit or dress and jacket with high heels. I choose the style that suits my shape and the colours that match my skin tone and hair. If you are not sure about these, there are organisations that can help you tailor your wardrobe for you like "Colour Me Beautiful".

Have your hair nicely styled, your nails manicured and your shoes well polished. I have found that even dealing with un-ruly youngsters is much easier when you are smartly dressed and have that air of authority about you.

# 4. Confidence

Confidence is vital on these occasions and this may be the bit that bothers you the most. Many people do not like the idea of standing in front of an audience. In fact it has been sited as one of the things people dread the most. But these fears can be overcome. Firstly remember that the audience is on your side. They want you to succeed and will help you all the way. They have chosen to listen to you rather than stay in the comfort of their own home so it is your duty to inform and entertain them.

You can build confidence by going into a state of deep relaxation and simply saying to your self "I am confident and I enjoy doing presentations". If you do this for about 5 minutes a day, every day for a couple of months you will be surprised at how much more confident you will become. If you want more information on this subject there are many books that cover it. I would recommend a simple one called The Lazy Man's Way to Riches written by Joe Karbo. Make sure you buy the original not the one written by his son Richard Nixon which is much more complicated.

## 5. Product

Finally you are looking to improve your pharmacy business, as well as increasing your standing, so try to link your talk to products and services that you can sell both on the night and in your shop at a later stage. As mentioned previously products like vitamins and minerals and aromatherapy oils are easy to transport, easy to demonstrate and always popular.

On a more health related topic you may choose to take on a selection of blood pressure machines, blood glucose and cholesterol testing kits or peak flow metres etc. to reinforce how pharmacists can help the group of patients you are talking about. Also try to incorporate details of the relevant services that you run e.g. MURs, Blood Pressure and glucose testing, vascular screening , etc.

Make sure you have price details, booking information and change with you. In fact taking another member of staff along with you to help with sales after the talk maybe a good idea. They can arrange the products and leaflets in to an attractive display before the presentation begins to encourage later sales.

# 6. Subject

We have already touched on the subject you may wish to choose but certainly to begin with, it may be wise to pick a topic that you are already pretty knowledgeable on. As you are a pharmacist and representing your business the obvious topics will be health related.

You may have a particular interest in a certain condition that has had an impact on your family, or an area of interest that you have developed over the years in your pharmacy or taken up a particular problem in your area. By basing your talk on a familiar topic you will feel more confident when presenting it and more able to answer any questions that arise at the end. Also, hopefully you will need to learn less in preparation and hence need less notes.

Make sure you research the topic thoroughly so that you have the latest studies and opinions about the best treatment for the conditions you have chosen. Be ready to answer questions but be prepared to admit if you don't know the answer. Take the questioners details and promise to contact them once you have found the answer. Make sure you do.

## 7. Why?

Running presentations is a way of increasing your standing in the community as an expert who's advice your audience can rely on. There will be many different groups in your area looking for new speakers to entertain their members. You can easily find them in your local paper, magazine or on the internet.

By giving an interesting and informative talk you will encourage more people to bring their queries and hopefully purchases to your pharmacy. By carefully choosing your subject you could encourage purchases on the night e.g. a talk on vitamins and food supplements or on aromatherapy.

When it is successful, you can get pictures taken and send them to the local press as a bit of PR, put them on your Facebook page, both of which may encourage further bookings, and on your message board in your shop.

## 8. Intro/Outro

It is important to have an introduction to explain who you are and what your qualifications are to the audience. If you are speaking to a group this is normally done by the chairperson but they will need the details from you. Think carefully how you want to be portrayed and don't be too modest. You have a University degree in pharmacy, many years experience dealing with various health concerns and the desire to prevent people getting ill.

When you have finished your talk again you need an outro. That is someone recapping on the mainpoints, explaining about the products on sale at the back of the room and where they can have a personal chat with you if they ever have any concerns. You may even consider giving out a flyer reinforcing details of the course with a map of your pharmacy and testimonials from your satisfied customers.

# Chapter Twelve: Sponsorship

"No one has ever become poor
from giving."
—Anne Frank

"We make a LIVING by what we GET,
but we make a LIFE from what we
GIVE."
—Winston Churchill

## 1. Who?

Sponsorship is another way to market your business that can be both enjoyable and benefit not only your pharmacy but help a local charity, sport team or even local arts project. You may find there are so many to choose from that it is difficult to decide which one.

So study the local press, talk to your staff, chat to your patients, maybe even have a competition to see who your customers think would be the best one for you to support. You may already be involved in an organisation that needs some financial help so you could promote your business whilst reaping the benefits in that area as well.

## 2. How?

How you sponsor will depend to a large extent on what you have decided to support. If it is a sport of some description then providing equipment or team uniforms with your company logo on may be the answer. If it is charity then running a series of events to raise money and awareness for the charity may be the way or if it is a local community project you might want to donate some of your staff hours so while they work on the project you continue to pay them.

You should record the games that the team play, the events to raise money, or the steps of the project, to display in your shop window. This will create interest among your customers and the feeling that your company are "good guys" there to do more than just make money.

Once you have made significant progress in your chosen field write a short article about the whole thing and send it along with the pictures you have taken to the local newspaper for them to publish thereby creating some free PR for your pharmacy. Run the story with pictures on your website or face book page and mention it on twitter. You could even send the details to the local radio station to get some coverage there.

## 3. Why?

The point of sponsoring is three fold.

Firstly, it means that you can be seen as supporting the local community, especially if it is a very local team, charity or project that you are choosing to help.

Secondly, it can be a source of PR that you can use in newspaper articles to raise the awareness of your company.

Finally, you and your staff can enjoy going to the sports matches, or charity events or watching the project develop which will increase the team spirit and commitment to your business.

## 4. Cost

It is important that you have a set budget for the amount you feel the business can afford to donate. It is very easy to get carried away and forget that the main purpose of your involvement is to improve the turnover of your business. So make sure that you can afford what you commit to.

Obviously you can help with more than just money. By organising and publicising events through your business you can raise money that is not directly coming from your coffers. Keep a track of the cash that you do donate as this becomes tax deductible and therefore technically cost the company far less.

If you donate hours rather than cash, keep a track of that as well.

## 5. Monitor

Monitor the progress of your chosen team, charity or project to ensure the money and time you are donating is being used wisely and to the benefit of the local community. You may want to delegate this to a member of staff who then reports back to the rest of the team.

As you are a business person the organisation you are helping may value some of your knowledge and contacts to help them get the most out of the donations of time and money they receive. Many volunteers do not necessarily have a good head for this sort of thing so this is another way you can support them.

LYNDA CHANIN

# Biography

Lynda and her husband Chris owned a small chain of community pharmacies based in the North West for 20 years. On the introduction of the pharmacy contract in 2005, they realised that many independent Pharmacists would struggle with the extra paperwork they would now have to complete.

They felt they could make use of Chris's computer expertise and Lynda's writing skills to fill this gap and become a virtual head office for these contractors. So they started their present company and have helped thousands of contractors reduce their paperwork and increase their profits.

They realised in 1995 they needed to become good at marketing, so they sought out world renowned experts in the field and studied under them. Since 1996 all the principles and practices they learned were put into practice, first of all in Chanin's Pharmacy and then for the past ten years in TheInformacist.com.

As time has gone by, it has become obvious that the vast majority of contractors, as well as many other small business owners, don't understand that marketing is the life blood of any business. Hence they have created this book to act as a guide on how to market your business.

# Testimonials

"Thank you for all your support, it's been fantastic!"

"You're a godsend."

"After talking to you I feel like a huge weight has been lifted off my shoulders already!"

—Jayesh Raja,
   Healthways Chemist,
   23 Apr 2014

"We learnt a lot [at the CPD13 Workshop]. We were fed like kings and also Chris and Lynda are a delight. [The CPD Workshop is] very good for the busy independent Pharmacist who has little time to do CPD. Giving up two Sundays of your time a year is a good way to achieve the required CPD for the year."

—H S Bains Senior and
   H S Bains Junior,
   9 Nov 2015

LYNDA CHANIN

16759372R00081

Printed in Great Britain
by Amazon